AF317008

This book belongs to
soccer superstar

_______________________!

The ABC's of Messi

Printed in the United States

ISBN# 9798325938726

KDP Publishing

Dedications

Thank you to my adoring wife who continues to support my dreams
and is with me every step of the way.
I love you!
To my three sons, Luke, Zack and Josh, who helped me brainstorm
relentlessly on the way to different events in the car.
You inspire and encourage me to keep pursuing greatness!
I love you all and you make me proud each and every day.
-Cameron

To Joey
Watching you grow has been so much fun!
I'm so proud of you and I can't wait to see all the things you accomplish.
I'll always be here for you no matter what.
-Mica

THE
ABC's
OF MESSI
An alphabet exploration of Lionel Messi
and popular soccer terms

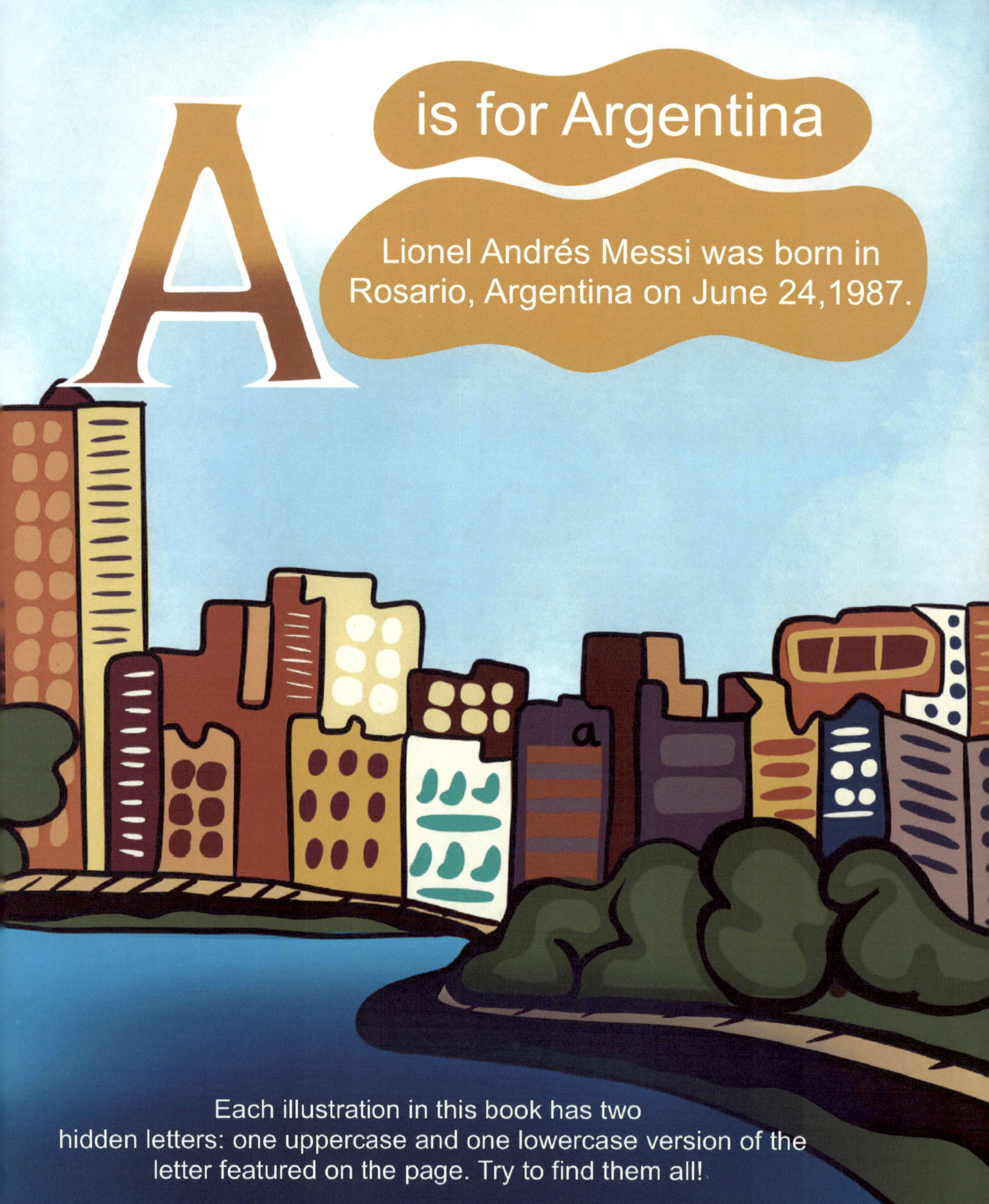

A
is for Argentina
Lionel Andrés Messi was born in Rosario, Argentina on June 24,1987.
Each illustration in this book has two hidden letters: one uppercase and one lowercase version of the letter featured on the page. Try to find them all!

B
is for Ballon d'Or Award
The Ballon d'Or award is awarded yearly to the best soccer player in the world and Messi has won it eight times.

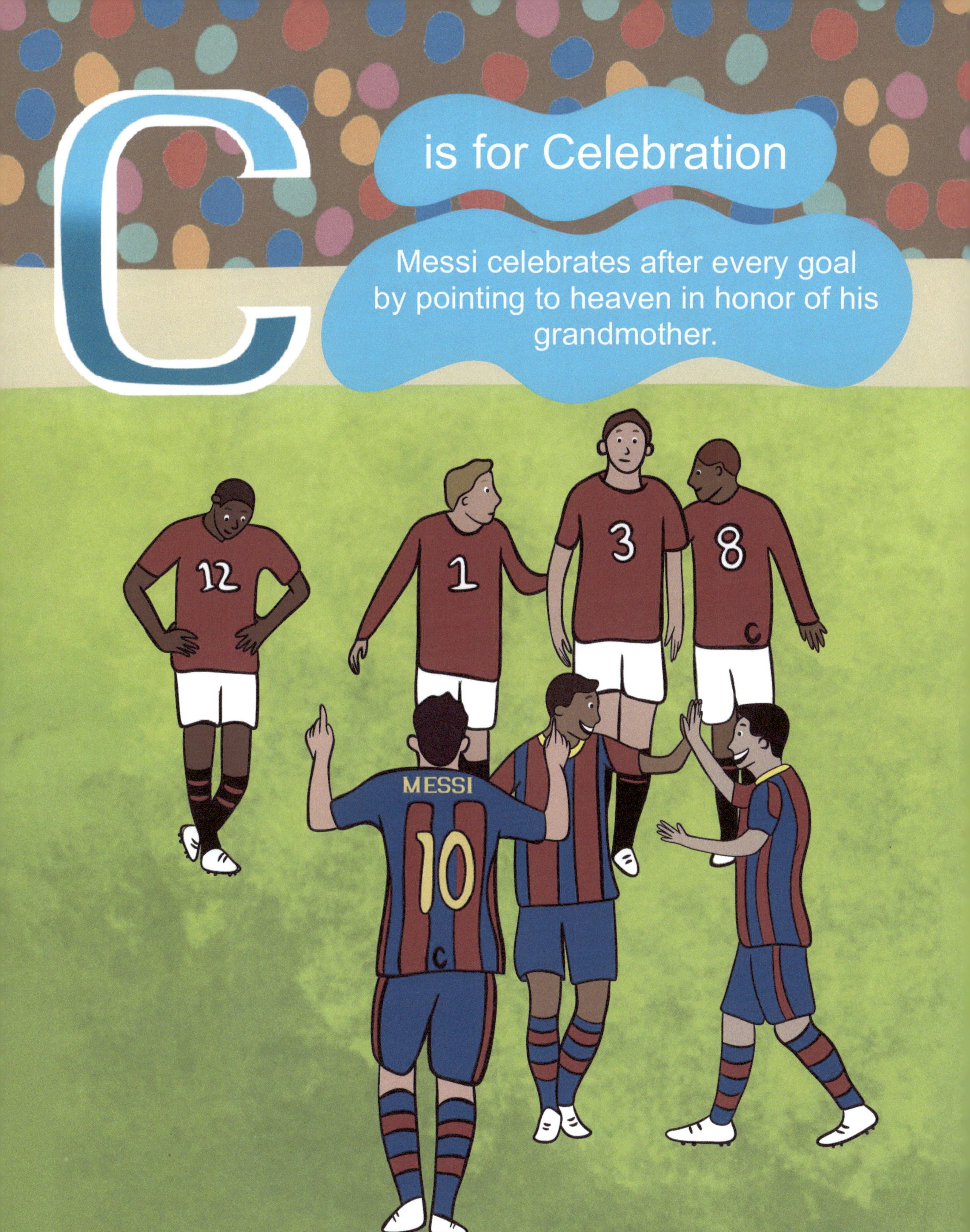

C

is for Celebration

Messi celebrates after every goal by pointing to heaven in honor of his grandmother.

D

is for Dribbling

Messi uses several different dribbling methods, such as using the inside, outside, and sole of his foot.

E

is for Exercise

Messi exercises almost every day to stay in top physical condition.

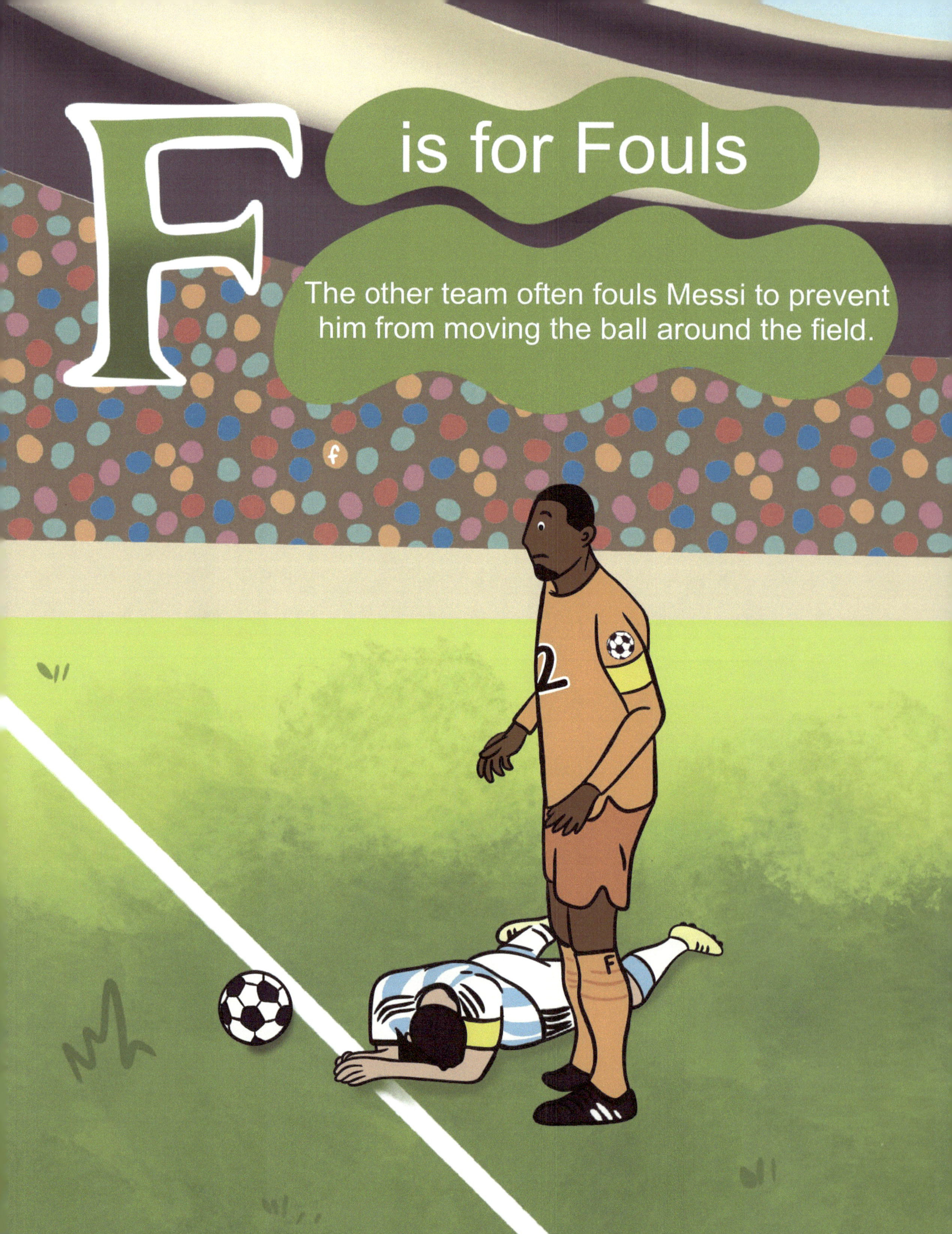

F
is for Fouls
The other team often fouls Messi to prevent him from moving the ball around the field.

G

is for Goals

Messi has scored over 800 goals, including both his Club and National team roles.

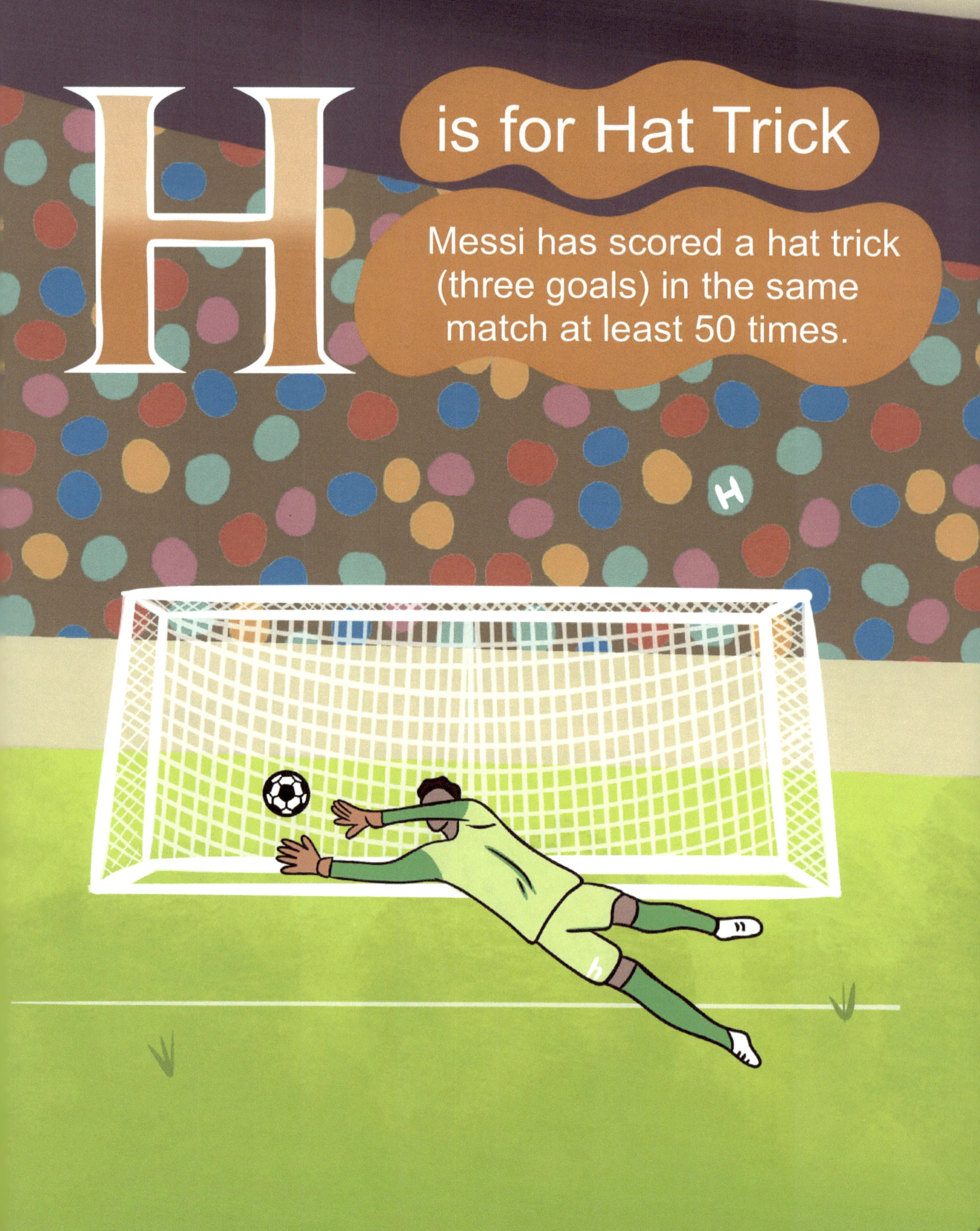

H
is for Hat Trick
Messi has scored a hat trick (three goals) in the same match at least 50 times.

I

Messi has suffered different injuries in his career, including thigh, knee, calf, foot, and bicep injuries.

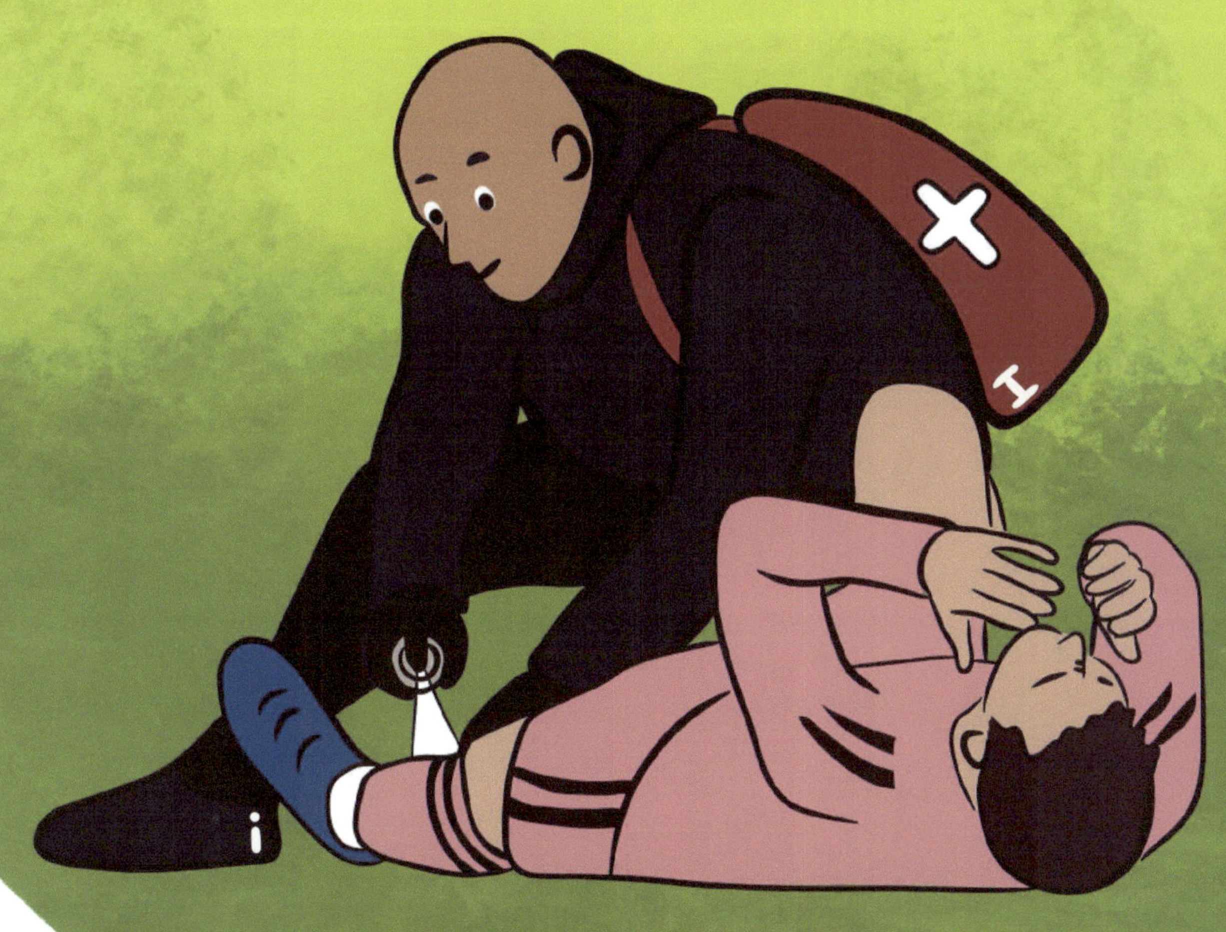

J

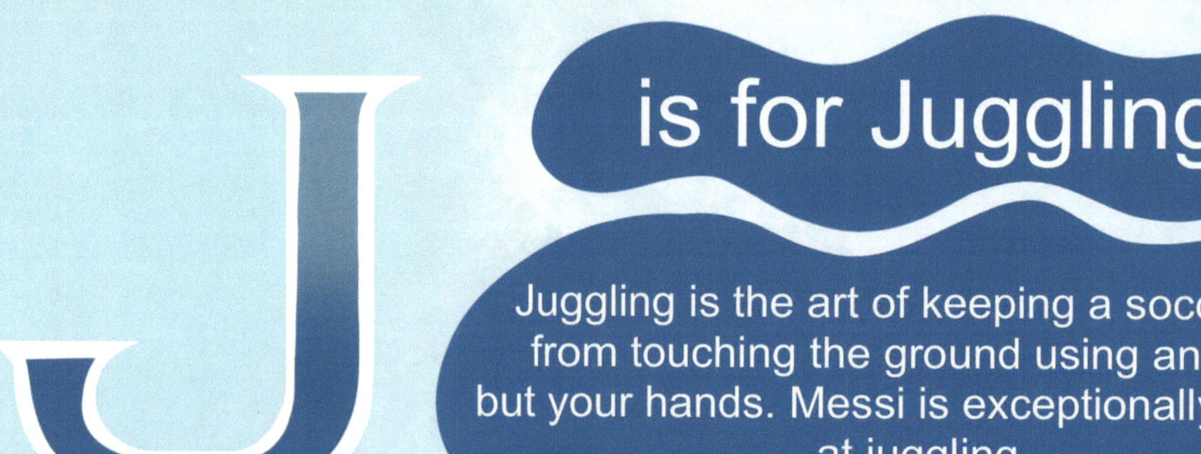

is for Juggling
Juggling is the art of keeping a soccer ball from touching the ground using anything but your hands. Messi is exceptionally talented at juggling.

K is for Kilos

Messi weighs approximately 67 kilograms (148 lbs.) and he can kick a ball an estimated 130 kilometers per hour (80 mph).

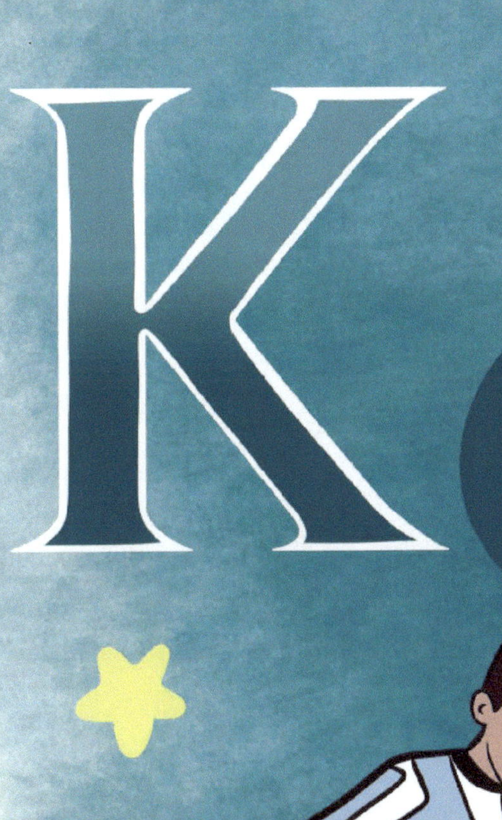

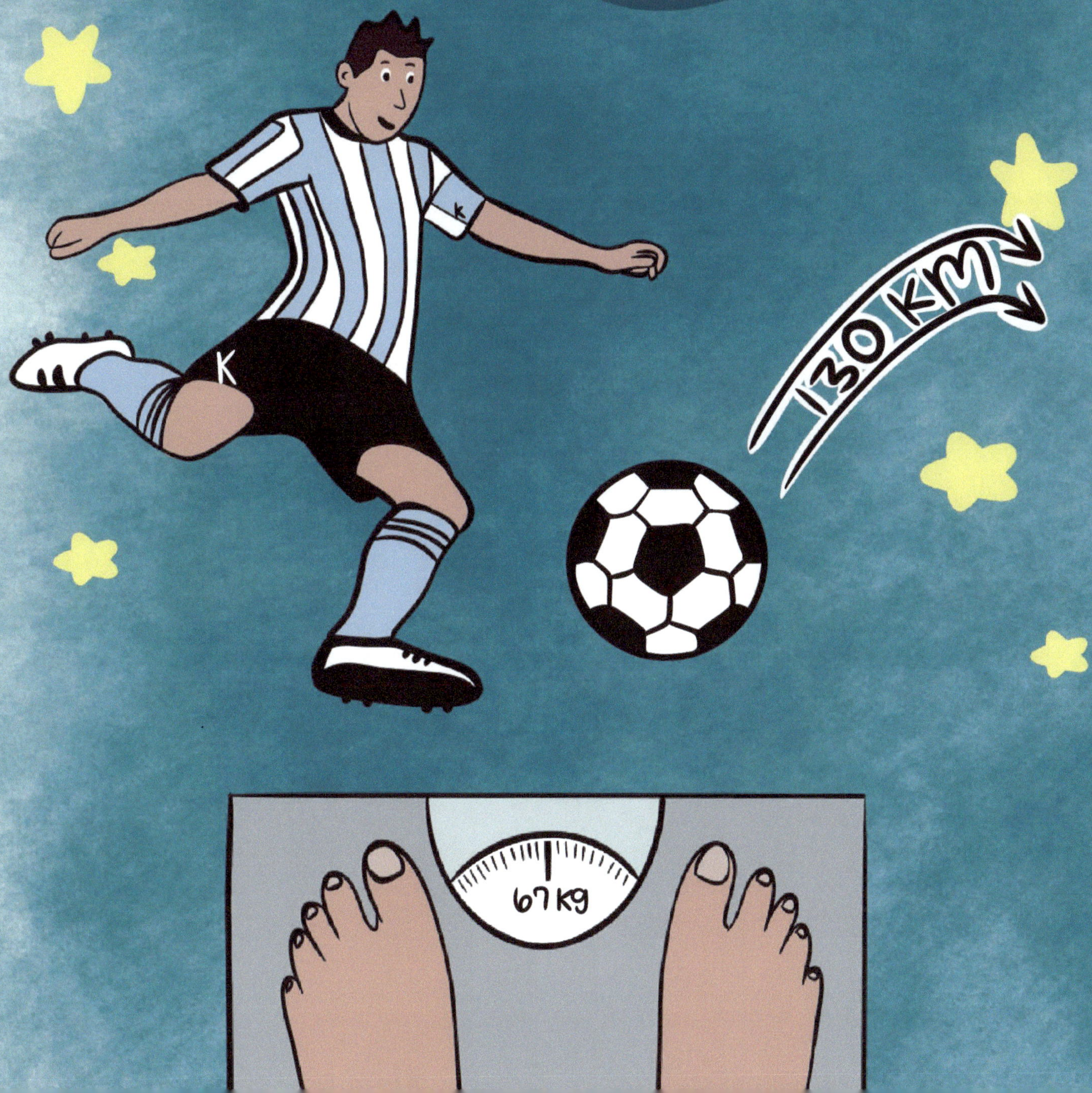

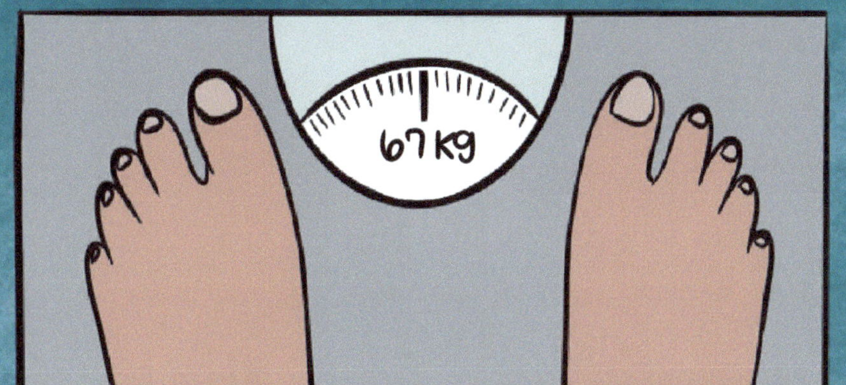

L

is for Leo Messi Foundation

The Leo Messi Foundation is dedicated to helping youth around the globe by providing assistance with healthcare, education and sports.

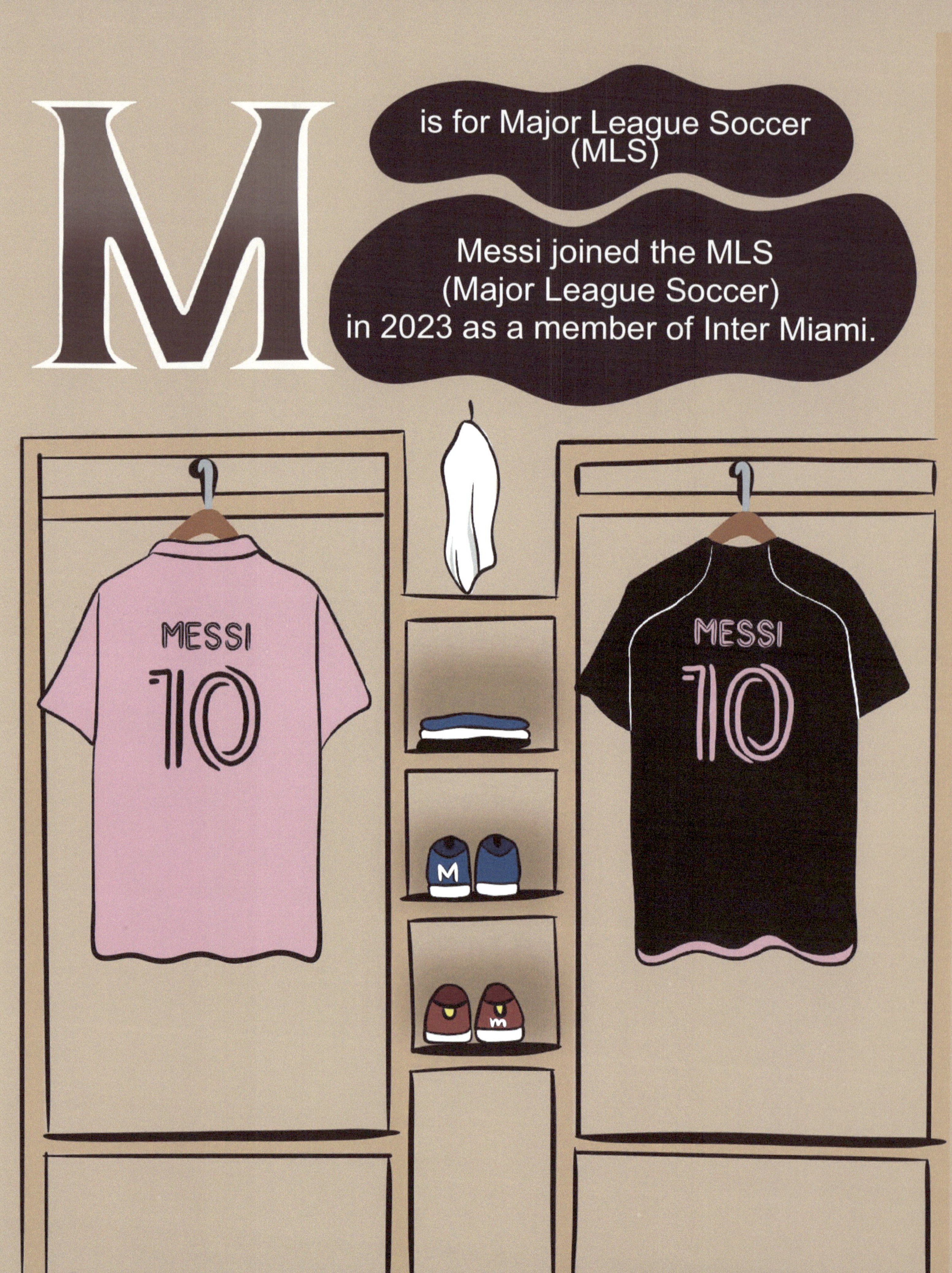
M
is for Major League Soccer (MLS)
Messi joined the MLS (Major League Soccer) in 2023 as a member of Inter Miami.
MESSI
10
MESSI
10

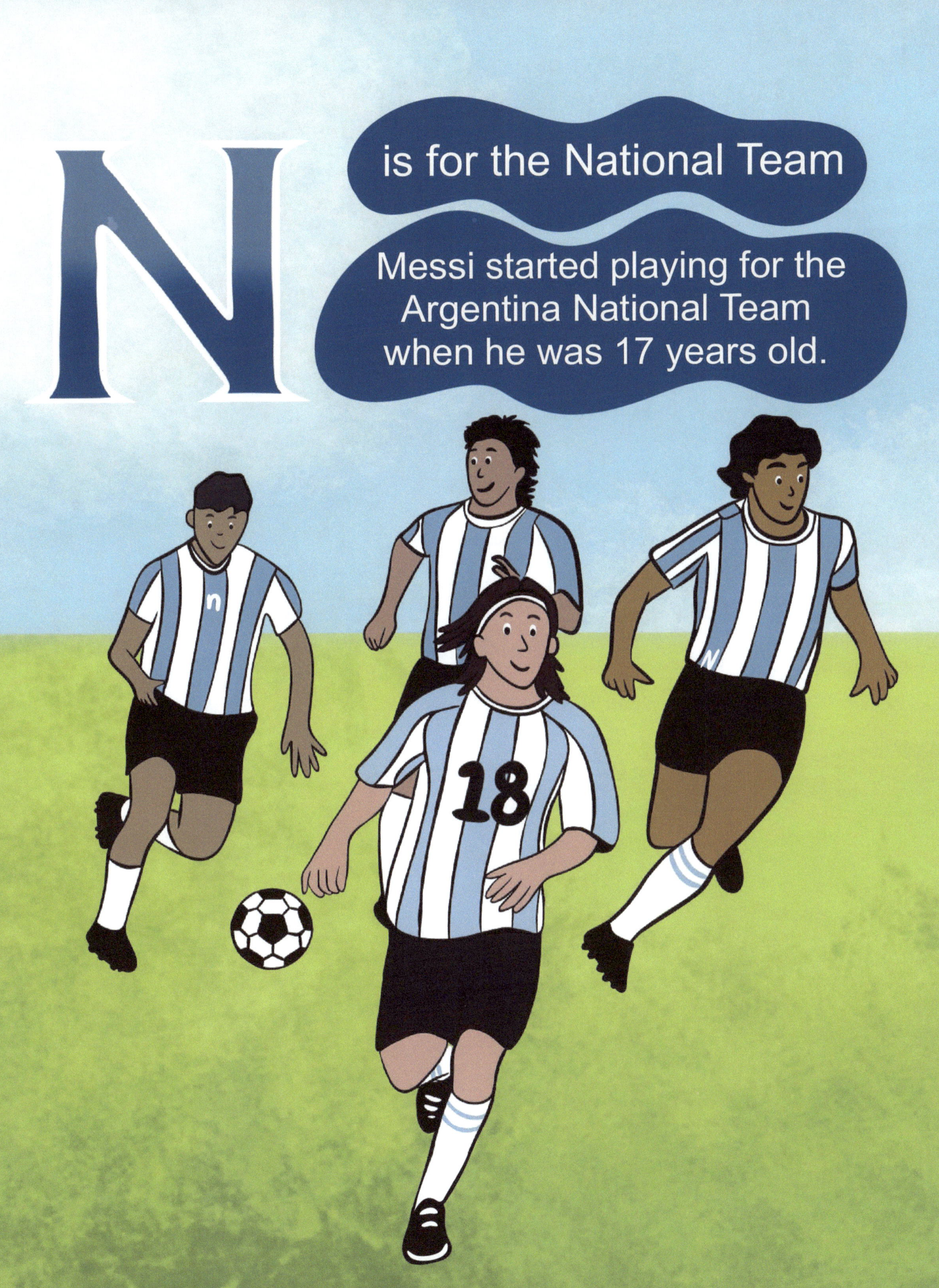
N
is for the National Team

Messi started playing for the
Argentina National Team
when he was 17 years old.

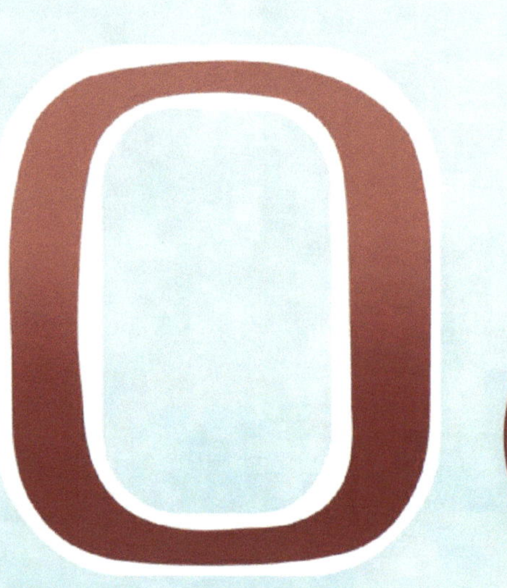

O is for Olympics

Messi played on the Argentinian Olympic soccer team in 2008 where they beat Nigeria to win the gold medal in Beijing.

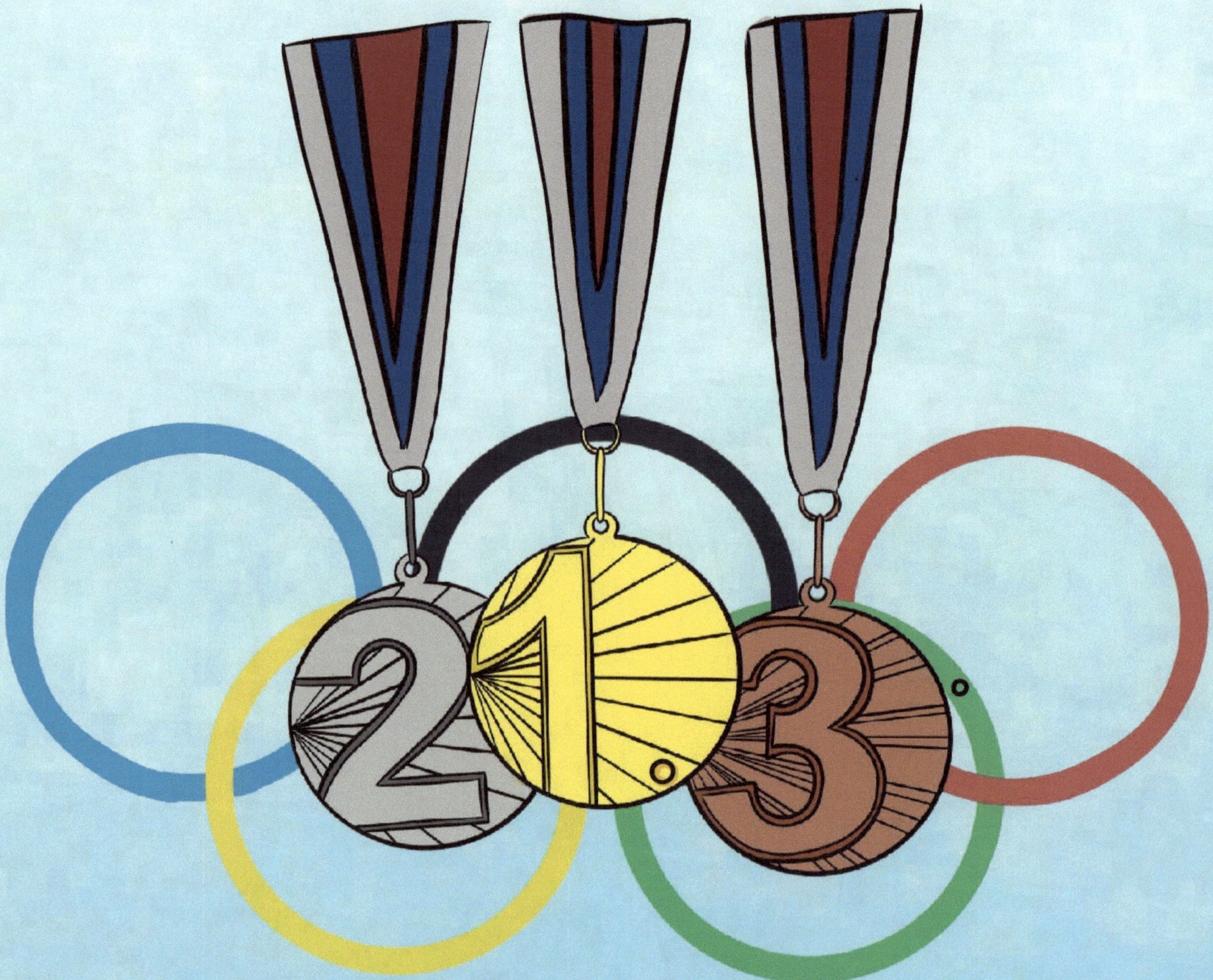

is for Penalty Kick
Messi has attempted over 130 penalty kicks and scored over 100 of them.

Q
is for Qatar
Messi led Argentina to win the 2022 World Cup in Qatar.
The game was played in Lusail Stadium against France.
Messi scored two goals and was named man of the match.

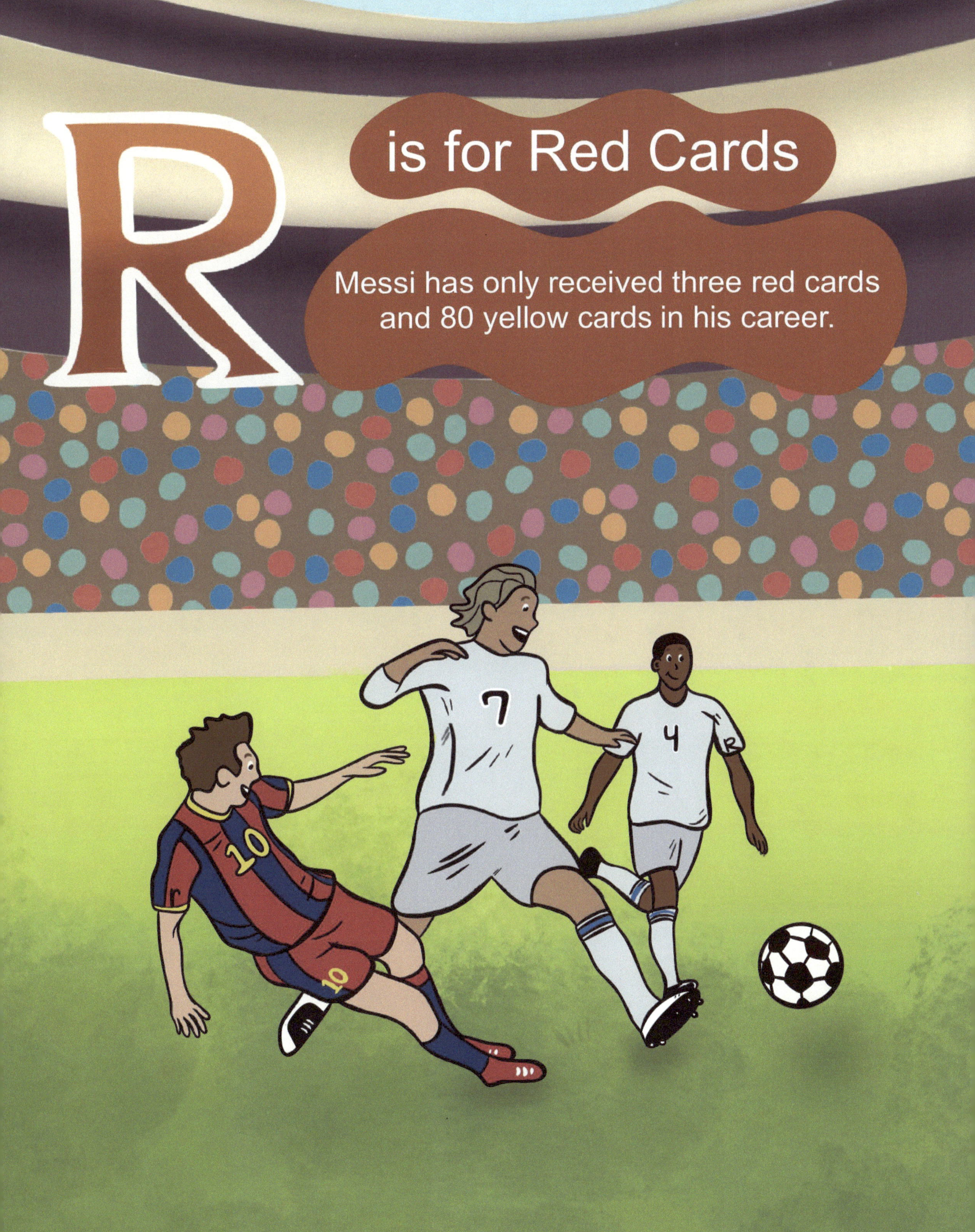
R
is for Red Cards
Messi has only received three red cards
and 80 yellow cards in his career.

S

is for Soccer

Fútbol is one of the most popular sports in the world, but is known as soccer in the United States.

T is for Three

Messi and his wife (Antonela Roccuzzo) have three sons together (Ciro, Mateo & Thiago).

U

is for Unique

Messi is considered unique because he is undersized compared to other soccer players, standing at 5'7" or 1.7m.

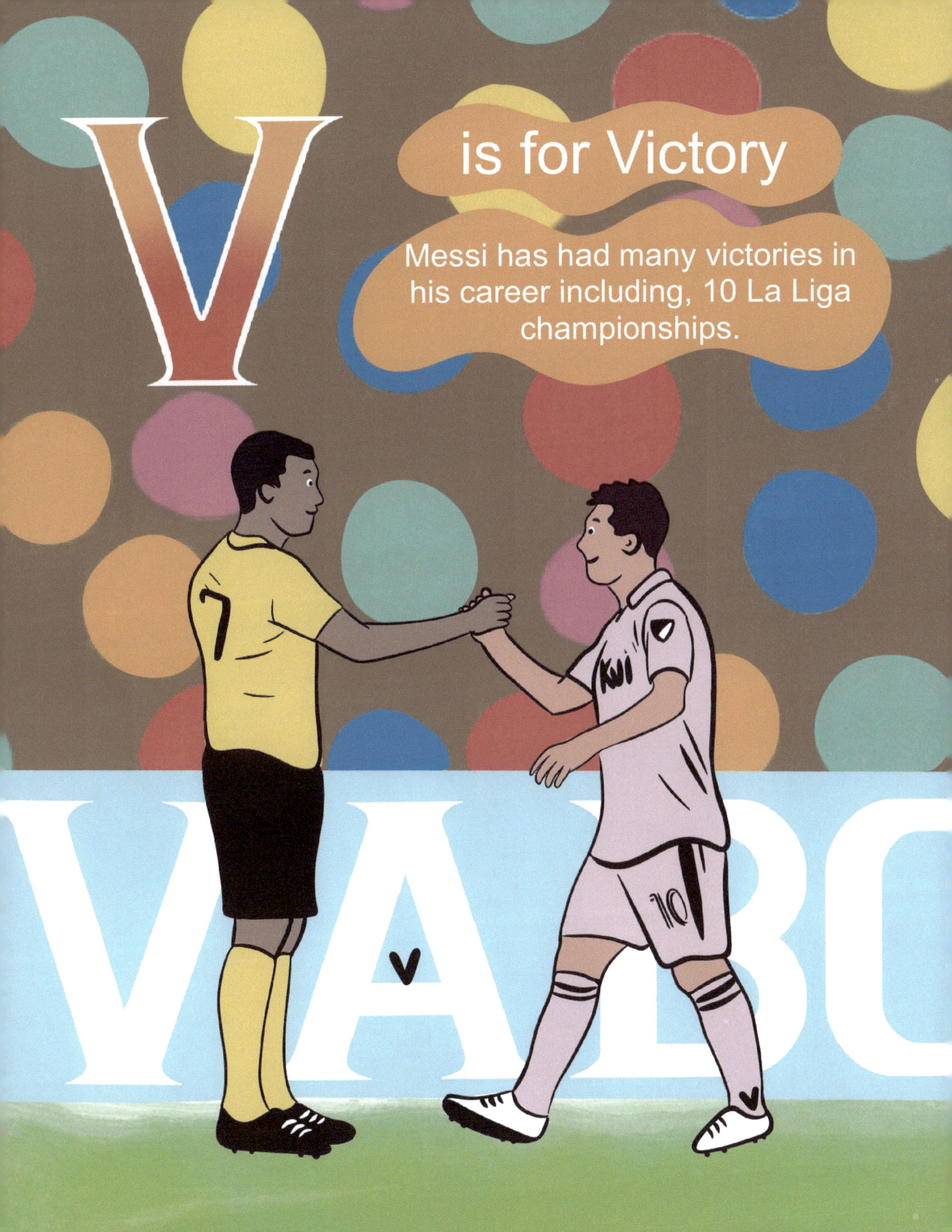

V
is for Victory
Messi has had many victories in his career including, 10 La Liga championships.

W is for Wembley Stadium

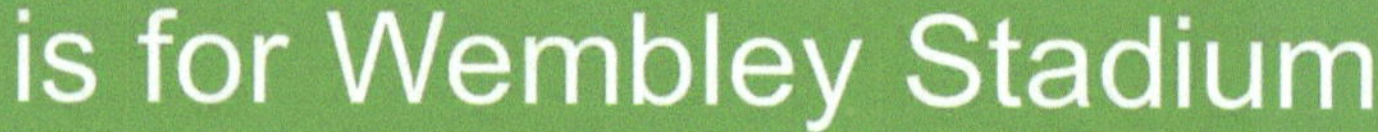

Messi has played at Wembley Stadium in London three different times and won each time. Wembley Stadium is a famous soccer venue built in 1923 and can hold roughly 90,000 fans.

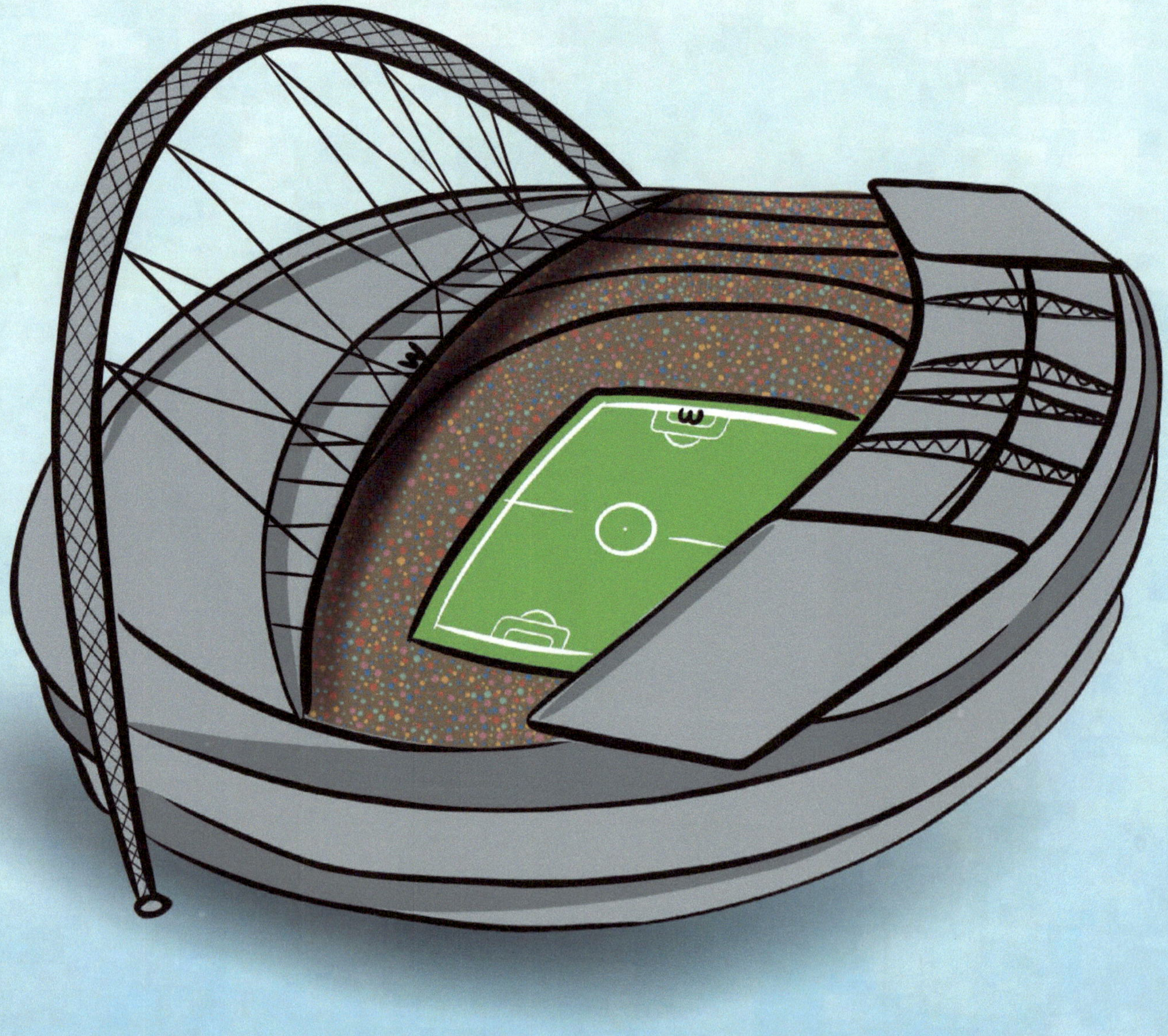

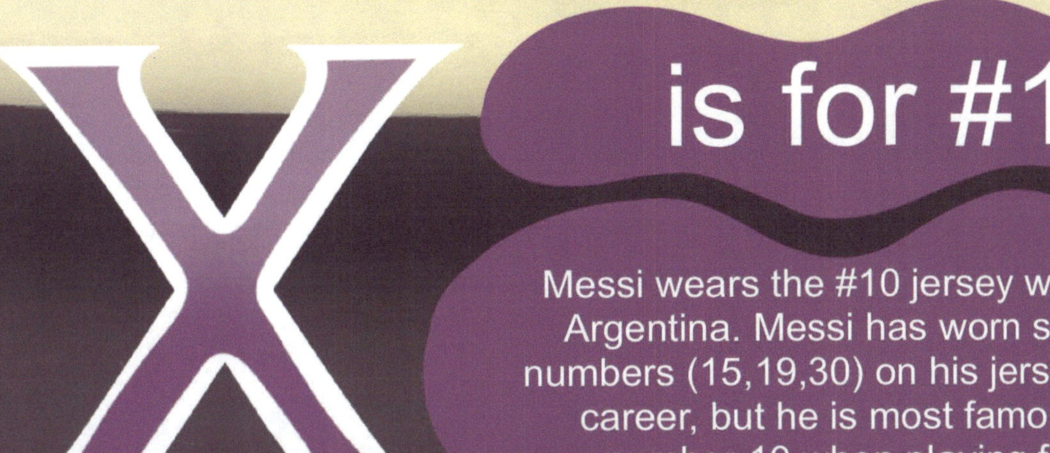

X is for #10

Messi wears the #10 jersey when he plays for Argentina. Messi has worn several different numbers (15,19,30) on his jersey throughout his career, but he is most famous for wearing number 10 when playing for Argentina.

Y is for Yards

Messi runs a lot during a match. On average, a soccer player will travel between 7,600-13,000 yards which is equivalent to 7 to 12 kilometers or 4 to 7 miles.

Z
is for Zero Percent
Zero (0%) chance any player is better than Messi.

The details in this book are based on information widely
found on the internet and were current
at the time of publishing in 2024.

To see more work by the illustrator, Mica Spence
please visit her website Etsy.com/shop/micacreatesco

Check out Cameron's other book on Amazon and Etsy -
The ABC's of Aggieland